THE EXCHANGE

THE EXCHANGE

AN INQUIRER'S BIBLE STUDY

JEFF MUSGRAVE

journeyforth®

Greenville, South Carolina

Cover Photo Credits: iStockphoto

The fact that materials produced by other publishers may be referred to in this volume does not constitute an endorsement of the content or theological position of materials produced by such publishers.

All Scripture is quoted from the Authorized King James Version unless otherwise noted.

The Exchange
Jeff Musgrave

Cover Design and Page Layout by Peter Crane

©2010 by BJU Press
Greenville, South Carolina 29614
JourneyForth Books is a division of BJU Press

Printed in the United States of America
All rights reserved

ISBN 978-1-60682-098-8

15   14   13   12   11   10   9   8   7   6   5   4   3

CONTENTS

INTRODUCTION

Many people are curious about God and would like to know Him better. Others think they know Him, but they do not really know the truth about Him. Others have a pretty good idea about Who He is but don't know for sure, or they are simply taking someone else's word for it. Through these four simple lessons you will grow in your understanding of Who God is, of what He desires from you, and of what He has done for you; and you will learn many other exciting truths directly from God's Word. Your Bible study leader will ask you to do a lesson at a time so that you can concentrate on it and carefully complete it. Each lesson includes Bible verses to read, questions to answer, a verse to memorize, and a practical assignment to complete. Follow the simple guidelines below to get the most out of each lesson.

LOOK

Read each verse thoughtfully. Ask God to speak to your heart through His Word (Romans 10:17 "So then faith [comes] by hearing, and hearing by the word of God").

LIST

Answer all the questions thoroughly based on the information given in the Bible verse. (Note: The answer is highlighted in **bold** print in most verses.) If you do not understand a question, leave it blank and ask your Bible study leader about it at your next meeting. Write down any questions or comments you have.

LEARN

Understand what God is teaching you from the Bible and how it applies directly to you. Memorize the verse at the end of each lesson. God will convince you of the truth of these verses as you meditate on them.

BELIEVE

God greatly desires that you become a participant in His
eternal life through depending on Him. Faith is not just
understanding and agreeing with someone; it is depending
on Him to do what He has said He will do. May God use
these simple lessons to show you this.

God will use your Bible study leader in your life to be a great
help to you as you inquire into Him. Write down the name and
phone number of your leader, and feel free to call him or her at
any time.

Name: _____

Phone: _____

LESSON 1

GOD IS HOLY AND MAN IS SINFUL

One of the most damaging notions to a real understanding of God and His relationship with man is the concept that God is a force or an energy source. Whereas God is indeed a force with which to be reckoned and the greatest power in the universe, He is so much more than that. He is a person! When we remove the concept of His personhood from our thinking, we take away the fact that He has likes and dislikes. We damage our ability to understand the whole concept of morality. We are left to define all the great questions of life by our own experience and intellect. This Bible study will not attempt to do that. Instead, this is an introduction to God as a person. Once you get to know Him as a person, you will have an understanding, or at least an access to an understanding, of these questions.

The Bible is a series of books from God to men in which He reveals Himself to mankind so that we may know Him.

1. Some people have the misconception that the Bible can be interpreted any way a person chooses. Notice what the Bible says about private interpretations.*

    *2 Peter 1:20–21—Knowing this first, that ᵃ**no prophecy of the scripture is of any private interpretation**. ᵇ**For the prophecy came not** in old time **by the will of man: but** ᶜ**holy men of God [spoke] as they were moved [carried along] by the Holy Ghost [Spirit]**.*

    a. What does the Bible say about private interpretations?

    _____

    b. Why is it wrong to make the Bible say what we want it to say?

    _____

    c. Who does this verse teach wrote the Bible?

    _____

The Bible was written by God's Holy Spirit, Who directed holy men to communicate His message to mankind. The "private interpretation" mentioned in this verse is probably not aimed at the reader so much as it is a record of how the Bible got to us. The Bible is not the private opinions of the human writers but the revelation of God. As such, there is a message from God that must be discovered without putting our own ideas or thoughts into it.

This is a **Bible** study. The purpose of this study is to lead you to a personal understanding of what the Bible says about God—to

---

*The Scriptures in this Bible study are taken from the King James Version (KJV) of the Bible. Some of the words are used differently in today's modern English and are followed by modern words in brackets [ ].

see it for yourself. A wise man once said, "The Bible is not hard to understand. It's just hard to obey." If at any point along the way you do not understand or agree, please do not hesitate to discuss your concern with your Bible study leader. You may not agree with everything the Bible says, but at least we should be able to come to an agreement about what the Bible teaches.

The Bible presupposes the existence of God and tells us from the very beginning Who He is.

> *Genesis 1:1—In the beginning God . . .*

In these four Bible lessons, we will examine four of God's greatest attributes—God is holy, God is just, God is loving, and God is gracious and merciful. The concept of God's holiness is mentioned nearly twice as often in the Bible as any of His other attributes.

2. The Bible gives us only two glimpses into the actual throne room of God. What phrase are the angels calling to each other in awe of His presence?

    *Isaiah 6:1–3—I saw also the Lord sitting upon a throne, high and lifted up, and his train [visible aura] filled the temple. Above it stood the seraphims [a type of angel]; each one had six wings; with twain [two] he covered his face, and with twain he covered his feet, and with twain he did fly. And one cried unto another, and said, **Holy, holy, holy, is the Lord of hosts: the whole earth is full of his glory**.*

---

3. The next glimpse into this room is in the last book of the Bible. The event described takes place at least 2,600 years

after the one in Isaiah 6. What phrase is still their ceaseless cry to each other?

Revelation 4:8—And the four beasts [angels] had each of them six wings about him; and they were full of eyes within: and they rest not day and night, saying, **Holy, holy, holy, Lord God Almighty, which was, and is, and is to come.**

The word *holy* means "separate" or "set apart." It has come to carry with it the idea of separation from the imperfections of sin. God is sinless. He has never done anything wrong.

4. In the Bible God declares Himself holy. What implication is placed on man as a result of God's holy nature?

    Leviticus 11:44—For I am the Lord your God: [you] shall therefore sanctify [set apart for service] yourselves, and **[you] shall be holy; for I am holy.**

---

5. What synonym did Jesus use to define God's holiness?

    Matthew 5:48—Be therefore **perfect,** *even as your Father which is in heaven is* **perfect.**

God is perfect! He is separate from everything else. God's holiness is best defined as His uniqueness. He is holy! There is no one else like Him. His holiness is described as "beautiful" many times in the Bible. His holy nature is gloriously beautiful. Another word used in close association with His holiness is *righteous.* You can count on the fact that God will always do the right thing. He is perfectly righteous. The idea is that of fulfilling a contract completely or perfectly. There may be times when we do not think that He is doing what is right, but He is holy. We are not. He always does what is right. He is not only the ruler of all and not answerable to you and me but He will always do the right thing. He has to. It is His character, His nature to do so; and He cannot violate His nature.

6. When a man doesn't know God, does it change Who God is and what He expects from man?

   Isaiah 45:5—I am the Lord, and there is none else, there is no God beside me: I girded [strengthened you], though [you] have not known me.

7. The problem that God's holiness causes for man is that we are not holy. Who does the Bible say is holy like God is holy?

   1 Samuel 2:2—There is none holy as the Lord: for there is none beside thee: neither is there any rock like our God.

Many people have heard of the Ten Commandments. What many do not know is that these ten basic laws are not just a set of rules to live by but are also a reflection of God's holy nature.

8. Read the record of the first giving of the Ten Commandments.

   Exodus 20:1–17—And God [spoke] all these words, saying, I am the Lord thy God . . .

   a. You shall have no other gods before Me.

   b. You shall not make unto you any graven image, or any likeness of any thing that is in heaven above, or that is in the earth beneath, or that is in the water under the earth: you shall not bow down yourself to them, nor serve them: for I the Lord your God am a jealous God, visiting the sin of the fathers upon the children unto the third and fourth generation of them that hate Me; and showing mercy unto thousands of them that love Me, and keep My commandments.

c. You shall not take the name of the Lord your God in vain; for the Lord will not hold him guiltless that takes His name in vain.

d. Remember the sabbath day, to keep it holy. Six days shall you labor, and do all your work: but the seventh day is the sabbath of the Lord your God: in it you shall not do any work,

e. Honor your father and your mother: that your days may be long upon the land which the Lord your God gives you.

f. You shall not kill.

g. You shall not commit adultery.

h. You shall not steal.

i. You shall not lie against your neighbor.

j. You shall not covet your neighbor's house, you shall not covet your neighbor's wife, nor his manservant, nor his maidservant, nor his ox, nor his donkey, nor anything that is your neighbor's.

Who gave us the Ten Commandments and what did He call Himself?

_____

What major attribute of God does the first commandment reflect?

_____

What attribute of God demands that we have no idols (anything more important to us than God) in our life?

_____

What do you think taking God's name "in vain" is?

_____

To take His name in vain is to use it flippantly or as an expletive like "Oh my _____!" (or "OMG").

Have you ever taken God's name in vain?

_____

What do you think "the Lord will not hold him guiltless" means?

_____

One of the aspects of God's holiness is not just that He dislikes sin but that He cannot tolerate it. It is not that He will not but that He cannot. He cannot deny any part of His perfect nature.

> *Habakkuk 1:13—Thou [God are] of purer eyes than to behold evil, and [cannot] look on iniquity [sin].*

You may struggle with the word *sin*. Many people define right and wrong differently. Remember we said that knowing God as a person clarifies some of these things. The Bible shows us God's definition of sin.

> *1 John 3:4— Sin is the transgression [breaking] of the law.*

Sin is not defined by my thoughts or by yours. It is defined by God's holy nature. When we sin, it is not simply that we have hurt someone or something; it is that we have offended God's holy nature.

How would you define "Honor your father and mother"?

To honor is not just obedience but having and displaying a sweet spirit at all times. Have you ever broken this command? There probably isn't a person alive who hasn't, especially in his teen years. The Bible calls that offense to God's holy nature "sin." You have broken God's law!

God created the family to teach us how to love and respect Him through learning to love and respect our parents.

God's command not to **murder** is a reflection of His love for human life. He created and sustains all that lives.

> *Colossians 1:16–17—For by him were all things created, that are in heaven, and that are in earth, visible and*

invisible . . . all things were created by him, and for him:
and he is before all things, and by him all things consist.

His command not to **commit adultery** is a reflection of His devotion to His own personal relationship with people and His commitment to the institution of marriage.

Hebrews 13:4—Marriage is honourable in all, and the
bed undefiled: but whoremongers [those who indulge in sex
before marriage] and adulterers God will judge.

His command not to **steal** shows Him as the provider of all material blessings.

Matthew 5:45—Your Father which is in heaven . . .
[makes] his sun to rise on the evil and on the good, and
[sends] rain on the just and on the unjust.

His command not to **lie** reflects His truthful nature. In fact, Titus 1:2 states that He cannot lie!

Numbers 23:19—God is not a man, that he should lie.

His command not to **covet** shows that, as God, He holds us responsible for what is in our hearts as well as what is in our conduct.

Have you ever lied? Have you ever committed adultery or stolen or coveted? You've broken God's law. You've offended His holy nature.

9.   Has anyone ever escaped this problem of sin?

*Ecclesiastes 7:20—**There is not a** just **man** upon earth,*
***that** [does] good, and [**sins**] **not**.*

Most of us are willing to admit that we have sinned, but many do not know that because of God's holy nature, sin disqualifies us from having a relationship with God.

10. What does this verse say is true about every person who has ever lived?

*Romans 3:23—For **all have** sinned, and **come short of the glory of God.***

Imagine for a moment that you and your Bible study leader are standing on the edge of the Grand Canyon. As you look across the eight-mile span to the other side, you are impressed not only by the distance to the other side but also by the nearly one-mile drop to the canyon floor below. What would happen if you had a contest to see which one of you could jump across? It would be foolish and futile. One of you would probably jump farther than the other, but you would both fall short of the other side. The Bible teaches us the same thing is true about our relationship with God. Some people may sin less than others, but all of us have sinned and have fallen short of God's standard of holy perfection.

11. How many lies does it take to keep a person out of God's heaven?

*Revelation 21:27—And there shall in no wise enter into it [heaven] **any thing that** [defiles], neither whatsoever [works] abomination, or [**makes**] **a lie**: but they which are written in the Lamb's book of life.*

Because God is holy, He cannot tolerate that which is not holy. We may think to ourselves that we can compensate for our sins by doing good things.

12. What does the Bible say that our "good things" are in the sight of our perfect God?

    Isaiah 64:6—But we are all as an unclean thing, and all **our righteousnesses [good things] are as filthy rags;** *and we all do fade as a leaf; and our iniquities [sins], like the wind, have taken us away.*

    _____

13. There is more to it than this, but if this were all you knew about God and men, who would make it to heaven?

    _____

14. If you were to die right now or five years from now, are you 100 percent sure that all your sins (past, present, and even future) are forgiven and that you have eternal life?

    _____

15. What do you believe a person must depend on to receive forgiveness of sins and eternal life in heaven?

    _____

    Think about this for a moment and record anything else that you think a person needs to depend on to get to heaven.

    _____

Lessons 3 and 4 deal with what the Bible has to say about these questions. If you feel as if you don't want to wait until then to find out, feel free to ask your Bible study leader to show you from the Bible now.

SUMMARY

In John 8:31–51 the Bible records an incident when Jesus was preaching to men about this subject; He told them that if they would listen to the truth, the truth would set them free. The men to whom He was speaking took exception to the thought that they needed freedom. They saw themselves as free to do whatever they wanted to do and as answerable to no man. Jesus replied, "[Truly] I say unto you, [Whoever commits] sin is the [slave] of sin."

You may be as those men and see yourself as free from the constraints of this kind of teaching. I once talked with a man on an airplane about this topic, and he somewhat sarcastically asked me, "How do you know this is true?"

I replied that the Bible is true and tells us more about ourselves than we can discover by personal observation. I told him the Bible teaches that all men are slaves to sin; I also told him that everyone has an area of his own life that he knows is wrong but can't change because he is enslaved to it. By way of personal application I told him, "Right now, there are things you do that you know are wrong to do and that you would like to stop doing, but you can't."

His glance in my direction told me that I had touched on something personal. He didn't even turn his head toward me, as if he suspected I was reading his mind. He responded by asking simply, "Everyone?"

I wasn't reading his mind. I had read the Bible. No man has the ability to overcome sin in his own nature, but Jesus has made it clear that He is the Truth and that He can free us from the guilt and the control of sin. What about you? Do you struggle with a sin that you know is wrong but you can't seem to quit? How do you deal with the guilt? Would you like to be free from sin and guilt once and for all? You can, and these Bible studies will lead you to the biblical truth of real freedom, so keep reading!

It is interesting. *The first step to this freedom is to admit that you are a slave.* That is, that you are a sinner who has offended God and you cannot solve this problem by yourself. Jesus told a story that is recorded in Luke 18:9–14. This was the description of the people to whom He was speaking: "Certain ones who trusted in themselves that they were righteous, and viewed others with contempt . . ." (NASB).

He said there were two men that went to the temple to pray. One of them was a very religious man, and the other was a tax collector. (The tax collectors of the day were despised for their personal greed and corruption.) The religious man stood in a prominent place with his eyes and hands lifted heavenward and prayed in his heart, "God, I thank You that I am not like other people: swindlers, unjust, adulterers, or even like this tax-gatherer. I fast twice a week; I pay tithes of all that I get."

The tax collector awkwardly stood some distance away and was not even willing to lift his face to heaven. His actions and stance told of the sense of guilt he carried. He prayed simply, "God be merciful to me, the sinner!"

Jesus continued to tell His listeners that the man who had humbled himself before God was the man who went away justified rather than the religious man who had exalted himself. Gaining freedom from sin is not about being better. It's too late for that, even if we could. It's about recognizing our need and admitting it to God!

APPLICATION

If you were going to talk to God about what you have learned in this Bible study lesson, what would you tell Him?

_____

_____

_____

MEMORIZE

Romans 3:23—For all have sinned, and come short of the glory of God.

PRACTICAL ASSIGNMENT

In the space provided record any ongoing questions about God you may have. Be sure to show them to your Bible study leader so that you will be able to discuss them together.

_____

_____

_____

_____

If you would like to study some on your own, try reading a chapter in the book of John each day. Ask God to speak to you as you read His book. Since He is real, He can do that. Don't expect

Him to speak out loud to you, but you can expect Him to speak to you. He promises that He will convince you in your heart of certain truths about Himself and about you. He will not speak in an audible voice, but you will have a growing awareness that what the Bible says is true! You may even sense a tugging or a squeezing in your heart. That is the Lord!

In the space remaining, also record any verses that seem to stand out to you or any questions you have as you read.

_____

_____

_____

_____

_____

_____

_____

_____

_____

_____

LESSON 2

GOD IS JUST AND MAN IS CONDEMNED

In lesson 1 we focused on the holiness of God. We learned that because God is holy, He cannot tolerate sin. This lesson focuses on His justice. This is not about a concept called justice but about a Person Whose nature is just. We will learn that because He is just, He cannot ignore or overlook our sin. As the just judge of all the earth, He must judge our sin.

1. In your own words describe the character of God shown in the following verse.

   *Deuteronomy 32:4—He is the rock, his work is **perfect**: for all his ways are **judgment**: a God of **truth** and **without iniquity, just** and **right** is he.*

   _____

He is the unchanging (rock), perfect God, Whose every action is just (declaring right and wrong). His very character is truth without any error, and He is always just and right. Remember,

He is perfect. He doesn't make any mistakes or commit any wrongs!

2. In the next lesson we will see that Jesus is God come to earth in a human body. What does this verse tell us about Him?

    *Hebrews 13:8—Jesus Christ **the same yesterday, and to day, and forever.***

    _____

He doesn't ever change. His character is the same in every situation.

3. How is Jesus described in this verse?

    *Acts 3:14—But [you] denied the **Holy** One and the **Just**.*

    _____

4. As a result of His just nature, what can you expect from His actions?

    *Psalm 111:7—The works of his hands are **verity [truth] and judgment [justice]; all his commandments are sure.***

    _____

He is a just God. Not only does He act justly Himself but He demands justice from men. When God gave His laws to His people, He was reflecting His holy nature, but some of His laws reflected His just nature as well.

5. Did God have one set of laws for foreigners and another for His own people? Why?

Leviticus 24:22—[You] shall have **one manner of law**, *as well for the stranger [foreigner], as for one of your own country:* **for I am the Lord your God.**

---

6. What words in this verse describe God's justice?

Genesis 18:25—Shall not the Judge of all the earth **do right [deal justly]**?

The topic of discussion in this passage is judgment, and the person who made this statement knew that he could count on God to deal with the judgment of the city in question in a just manner.

7. A covenant is a lasting promise or vow made with an oath. How does God's just nature affect His covenants positively and negatively?

Deuteronomy 7:9–10—Know therefore that the Lord [your] God, he is God, the **faithful God, which [keeps] covenant** *and mercy with them that love him and keep his commandments to a thousand generations; and [repays]* **them that hate him** *to their face, to destroy them: he will not be slack to him that hate him, he will repay him to his face.*

Positively _____

Negatively _____

His unchanging, just nature is a blessing. We can look at every promise in the Bible and know that God will keep each one because He is just. However, His just nature is also a terrifying truth because He must repay every sin and every man is a sinner.

8. We learned in lesson 1 that the first impact of seeing God on His throne is His holiness. What else is true about the atmosphere around the throne room of God?

   *Psalm 89:14—**Justice and judgment are the habitation [environment] of [Your] throne**: mercy and truth shall go before [Your] face.*

   _____

9. What is God prepared to do?

   *Psalm 9:7–8—But the Lord shall endure forever: **he [has] prepared his throne for judgment**. And he shall judge the world in righteousness, he shall minister judgment to the people in uprightness.*

   _____

10. What does God say will happen to the person who sins?

    *Ezekiel 18:20—**The soul that [sins], it shall die.** The son shall not bear the iniquity of the father, neither shall the father bear the iniquity of the son: the righteousness of the righteous shall be upon him, and the wickedness of the wicked shall be upon him.*

    _____

11. How many sins is God prepared to allow into heaven?

    *Revelation 21:27—And **there shall in no wise enter into it [heaven] any thing that [defiles]**, neither whatsoever works abomination, or [makes] a lie: but they which are written in the Lamb's book of life.*

    _____

12. Who is the ultimate judge of equity?

> *Ezekiel 33:20—Yet [you] say, The way of the Lord is not equal. . . . I [God] **will judge** you every one after his ways.*

> *Psalm 7:8—The Lord shall judge the people . . .*

---

13. Someone might say, "I've done many good things in my lifetime, or I've been a very religious person. Surely God will look at me differently because of my good works." What does God say about the way He judges?

> *Deuteronomy 10:17–18—For the Lord your God is God of gods, and Lord of lords, a great God, a mighty, and a terrible, **which [regards] not persons**, nor [takes] reward [bribes]: He [executes] judgment [justice].*

> *Acts 10:34—**God is no respecter of persons.***

---

14. Someone might say, "But I didn't know about this!" What does the Bible say about this plea?

> *Proverbs 24:12—If [you say], Behold, we knew it not; [does] not he [God] that [ponders] the heart consider it? and he that [keeps your] soul, [does] not he know it? and **shall not he render to every man according to his works?***

The concept of every man's being judged "according" to his own works occurs many times throughout the Bible. God will hold every one of us accountable for the specific sins that we have done—not any that others have done, but all that we have done—whether we have been aware of those sins or not.

One person might say, "That's not fair." There is a difference between justice and fairness. Frankly, fairness is most often determined by feelings, and justice is determined by facts. Most people who are in prison are there justly. They broke some law of the land and were held accountable to that law. They may not feel that they have been treated fairly, but that does not change the fact that justice has been served. Justice is not defined by what we feel or want but by fixed laws or facts. One of the definitions of *justice* in Webster's dictionary is "the administration . . . of law." Just as God is holy and cannot tolerate sin, He is also just and cannot ignore it.

Another might say, "I thought God was a loving God. How can He judge men like that?" Imagine a judge presiding over a murder trial. A mountain of evidence proves that the defendant is guilty.

Would justice be served if the judge chose to overlook the obvious guilt and acquit the murderer?_____
If the guilty man was the judge's brother and he loved him very much, would it be just if the judge chose to overlook his guilt and acquit him? _____
His love for the guilty would not change the demand for justice!

If God were to overlook **your** sin, would that be justice? _____
God, by His very nature is bound by justice. He must judge our sin.

15. What does the Bible say we deserve because of our sin?

    *Romans 6:23—For the wages of sin is **death**.*

_____

16. What kind of death is named in this description of the final judgment of men?

    *Revelation 20:11–14—And I saw a great white throne,
    and him that sat on it, from whose face the earth and the*

*heaven fled away; and there was found no place for them.
And I saw the dead, small and great, stand before God;
and the books were opened: and another book was opened,
which is the book of life: and the dead were judged out of
those things which were written in the books, according to
their works. And the sea gave up the dead which were in
it; and death and hell delivered up the dead which were in
them: and they were judged every man according to their
works. And death and hell were cast into the lake of fire.*
This is the second death.

This second death is most commonly called hell. Jesus spoke
more about hell than He did about heaven during His earthly
ministry. Some have determined that hell is not a place but a state
of mind or a figment of one's imagination.

17.   Note the words the Bible uses to describe this awful place
of judgment. Does it sound like a real place to you?

*Hebrews 9:27—And as it is appointed unto men once to
die, but after this the **judgment**.*

*Matthew 25:41, 46—Then shall he say also unto them
on the left hand, Depart from me, [you] cursed, into
everlasting fire, prepared for the devil and his angels. . .
. And these shall go away into everlasting punishment: but
the righteous into life eternal.*

*Luke 3:17—. . . will burn with **fire unquenchable**.*

Read this story told by Jesus. Doesn't hell sound like a real place
that should be avoided at all cost?

*Luke 16:19–24—There was a certain rich man, which
was clothed in purple and fine linen, and fared [lived]
sumptuously [splendidly] every day: and there was a certain*

beggar named Lazarus, which was laid at his gate. . . .
*And it came to pass, that the beggar died, and was carried
by the angels into Abraham's bosom: the rich man also
died, and was buried; and in hell he lift up his eyes,* **being
in torments,** *and [saw] Abraham afar off, and Lazarus
in his bosom. And he cried and said, Father Abraham,
have mercy on me, and send Lazarus, that he may dip the
tip of his finger in water, and cool my tongue; for* **I am
tormented in this flame.**

As terrible and unthinkable as it is, hell is a real place!

18. Who does the Bible say will go into the lake of fire?

*Revelation 21:8—But the fearful, and unbelieving, and
the abominable, and murderers, and whoremongers, and
sorcerers, and idolaters,* **and all liars shall have their
part in the lake** *which [burns] with fire and brimstone:
which is the second death.*

That's a rough list and probably you haven't done most of those
things, but **have you ever told a lie**? How many murders does a
man have to commit before he becomes a murderer? Only one.
How many lies does a person have to tell before he becomes a
liar? Only one.

You may be saying, "Wait a minute! I thought God is a God of
love! How could a loving God do this?" Don't forget! God cannot
deal with man in a way contrary to His nature. He is holy! He
cannot tolerate sin. He is just! He cannot overlook sin. He must
judge it. He has provided another way that satisfies His holiness,
justice, and His love. This is the GOOD NEWS *The Exchange* is
designed to tell you about. Lesson 3 deals with this good news,
but before we move on, answer this most important question.

19. Based on what we have learned from the Bible so far, if you were to die right now, where would you go?

_____

If you had to honestly answer "hell," are you concerned about this?

_____

Please don't be angry with God. Remember, He is just. He is doing what is right.

20. Who is at fault in this situation?

*Nehemiah 9:33—Howbeit [You God are] just in all that is brought upon us; for {You have] done right, but **we have done wickedly**.*

_____

21. Dear friend, God doesn't want you to go to hell! What does He want you to do right now?

*Ezekiel 18:32—For I have no pleasure in the death of him that [dies, says] the Lord God: wherefore **turn yourselves, and live**.*

_____

Lessons 3 and 4 deal with what one has to do to "turn and live." If you feel you don't want to wait until then to find out, feel free to ask your Bible study leader to show you from the Bible now.

SUMMARY

You might say, "This is frightening. Why would you focus on this?" Look at it this way. If I were standing on a dark mountain highway late on a stormy night and knew there was a bridge out just around the corner and I saw a car unknowingly speeding toward impending doom, what should I do? I must stop the car to warn the people inside of their danger! The danger of hell is real and the warning is necessary!

I know a woman who knew these truths but procrastinated about making a decision regarding them. When she was twenty-five, she woke up one morning having dreamed about being in hell. That was all it took! Fearful, she called her brother and begged him to come immediately to help her. When he arrived, she prayed the prayer of the tax collector in lesson 1, and the fear that was so real a minute before rolled away and God gave her a lasting peace. She is now the mother of three, continues to serve the Lord, and never worries about her sin problem and its penalty.

Jesus has provided a way for cleansing and complete forgiveness. Luke 19:10 teaches that Jesus is looking for people who will humble themselves before Him to save them from their doom. "For the Son of man [Jesus] is come to seek and to save that which was lost."

Early one morning during Jesus' earthly ministry, some men dragged a weeping woman into the courtyard where He was teaching. They wanted to use her to catch Him in a trap. They told Him that she had been caught in the very act of adultery and that the law demanded that she be stoned to death. They asked Him, "What do you have to say about that?"

They knew that if He spoke contrary to the Jewish law, the Jews would lose respect for Him. If He condemned her, He would break the Roman law that forbad executions without Rome's consent and He would be arrested. There was a silent moment as the crowd of triumphant men waited for Him to walk into their inescapable trap.

Unexpectedly, He stooped down and began to write in the dust with His finger. No one knows for sure what He wrote, but in that He knows everything, perhaps He began to list all of their hidden sins. He rose then and responded to their continued demand for an answer. "Which one of you is without sin? Let him be the first to throw a stone at her."

Then He silently stooped to write again, perhaps writing their more grievous and embarrassing sins. The Bible records that being convicted in their consciences about their own sins, they began to slip out one by one, beginning from the oldest to the youngest, until there was not one of them left but the accused woman.

Jesus rose from the ground and asked her, "Where are the witnesses against you? Is there no one to accuse you?"

With her head bowed to the ground in humility she answered, "No man, Lord," implying that she respected Him as judge and that her own heart told her that she was guilty. Jesus readily accepted her humble response and admonished her to "go and sin no more."

Jesus, the just Lord, was not willing to overlook the sins of her accusers and was willing to forgive her sins. Indeed, today He cannot overlook our sins, but He will gladly forgive those who will "turn and live."

APPLICATION

If you were going to talk to God about what you have learned in this Bible study, what would you tell Him?

_____

_____

_____

MEMORIZE

*Romans 6:23—The wages of sin is death; but the gift of
God is eternal life through Jesus Christ our Lord.*

PRACTICAL ASSIGNMENT

In the space provided record any ongoing questions about God
you may have. Be sure to show them to your Bible study leader so
that you will be able to discuss them together.

_____

_____

_____

_____

_____

If you would like to study some on your own, try reading a
chapter in the book of John each day. If you started this already,
continue in the book of John. Ask God to speak to you as you
read His book. Since He is real, He can do that. Don't expect
Him to speak out loud to you, but you can expect Him to speak
to you. He promises that He will convince you in your heart of
certain truths about Himself and about you. It will not be an
audible voice, but there will be a growing awareness that what the

Bible says is true! You may even sense a tugging or a squeezing in your heart. That is the Lord!

In the space remaining, also record any verses that seem to stand out to you or any questions you have as you read.

_____

_____

_____

_____

_____

_____

_____

_____

_____

LESSON 3

GOD IS LOVING AND MAN IS LOVED

What we have learned about God in lessons 1–2 is awesome and true but is bad news for mankind. God is holy and cannot tolerate our sin. He is just and cannot overlook our sin. Our sinful nature is offensive to His nature, and we are separated from Him and His perfection. If this were all there was to His nature, we would all be doomed. But there is more! The Bible teaches that "God is love" (1 John 4:8). While God cannot deny His nature and embrace us in our sin, He has provided a way for us to be close to Him because of His strong love for us. This perfect way to God satisfies His holiness and justice. Lesson 3 shows His great love and provision He has made for us to enter into an eternal love relationship with Him.

1. We have all experienced the need for love. Does prosperity satisfy this need?

   *Ecclesiastes 5:10—**He that [loves] silver shall not be satisfied** with silver; nor he that [loves] abundance with increase: this is also vanity [empty living].*

2. Note the picture this proverb paints for us. Maybe you remember sharing a sparse meal with someone dear to you or one shared in silence or bitter arguing. Recall a time this picture was true in your life? Briefly record your experience.

    Proverbs 15:17—Better is a dinner of herbs [sparse meal] **where love is***, than a stalled ox [feast] and* **hatred therewith***.*

    _____

    _____

    _____

What would you say is the most powerful motivation to the human mind? Some would say fear, citing the body's almost superhuman reactions to fear as evidence. Others would say greed or hunger for power, citing the inhumane atrocities that have been perpetrated because of these motives. I would propose that the greatest human motivation is love. Men have left all they have ever known and loved for love of country and freedom. I have a dear friend who ran into her burning house to save the life of her two-year-old daughter, resulting in burns to 65 percent of her body.

3. First Corinthians 13 is known as the Love Chapter. What does the last verse of that great chapter say about love?

    1 Corinthians 13:13—And now [abides] faith, hope, charity [love], these three; but **the greatest of these is charity [love]***.*

Love is the most ennobling human grace because man reflects the character of his Creator. God is love, and He created man with a capacity and a need for love.

4. What did God say about His love for men, and what has He done about it?

    *Jeremiah 31:3—The Lord [has] appeared of old unto me, saying, Yea, **I have loved [you] with an everlasting love: therefore with lovingkindness have I drawn [you]**.*

    *Hosea 11:4—**I [God] drew them** [my people] with cords of a man, **with bands of love**.*

Even now, God is drawing you to Himself in love. Won't you open your heart to Him? God created all of us with an appetite for His love that cannot be satisfied with anything but an intimate love relationship with Him.

5. How is God described in this passage?

    *2 Corinthians 13:11—Finally, brethren . . . the **God of love and peace** shall be with you.*

6. Is God's love available to you?

    *2 Corinthians 13:14—The grace of the Lord Jesus Christ, and **the love of God**, and the communion of the Holy Ghost [Spirit], **be with you all**. Amen.*

    *2 Thessalonians 3:5—And **the Lord direct your hearts into the love of God**.*

7. In your own words write the benefits of His love described in these verses.

   Ephesians 3:19—And to know **the love of Christ, which [passes] knowledge, that [you] might be filled with all the fulness of God.**

   2 Thessalonians 2:16—Now our Lord Jesus Christ himself, and God, even our Father, which [has] **loved us,** *and [has]* **given us everlasting consolation [comfort] and good hope through grace.**

   _____

   _____

8. Whom does God love?

   Deuteronomy 23:5—The Lord [your] God **loved** *[you].*

   _____

If you said "everyone," you are right, but the point is that He loves *you*, personally!

9. According to the Bible, from where does our human capacity to love come?

   1 John 4:19— **We love** *him [God],* **because he first loved us.**

   _____

10. Does the Bible indicate that God wants men to be separated from Him for eternity?

    *2 Peter 3:9—***The Lord is** *not slack concerning his promise, as some men count slackness; but is longsuffering to us-ward,* **not willing that any should perish,** *but that all should come to repentance.*

*1 Timothy 2:4—**Who [God] will have all men to be saved**, and to come unto the knowledge of the truth.*

God's love and God's holiness and justice seem to be in conflict regarding man's status. Yet they cannot be because God is perfect. The great love of God led Him to the most amazing act of love ever. He sent His own dear Son to bear our sin penalty for us.

11. What does the Bible say about true friendship?

   *Proverbs 17:17—**A friend [loves] at all times.***

---

12. Whom do you think this verse is talking about?

   *Proverbs 18:24—**There is a friend** that [sticks] closer than a brother.*

Jesus said of Himself in John 15:13, "**Greater love [has] no man than this**, that a man lay down his life for his friends."

13. What was Jesus called by the men of His own time?

   *Matthew 11:19—The Son of man [Jesus] came eating and drinking, and they say, Behold . . . **a friend of publicans [despised tax collectors] and sinners.***

---

14. What is the motive God gives for delivering His people in these verses?

   *Isaiah 38:17—Behold, for peace I had great bitterness: but [You God have], **in love to my soul** delivered it from the* *pit of corruption: for [You have] cast all my sins behind [Your] back.*

*Isaiah 63:9—In all their affliction he [God] was afflicted [grieved] . . . **in his love and in his pity** he redeemed [purchased out of the slave market and set free] them; and he bare them, and carried them.*

---

15.   What does the Bible say God's love motivated Him to do?

*John 3:16—For God so loved the world, that **he gave his only begotten Son**, that whosoever [believes] in him should not perish, but have everlasting life.*

*Romans 5:8—But God [commended, stretched forth] his love toward us, in that, while we were yet sinners, **Christ died for us**.*

God is loving and has reached out to us, but even in His love God cannot do anything that would violate the rest of His nature. It was through the gift of Jesus that He provided a way for us to be close to Him that satisfies His holy/just nature.

16.   Who would you say Jesus is?

If you said, "the Son of God," you are right, but think about this—God calls all true Christians His sons. Is Jesus different from them? YES!

17.   Who does this verse say Jesus is?

*Matthew 1:23—Behold, a virgin shall be with child, and shall bring forth a son, and they shall call his name Emmanuel, which being interpreted is, **God** with us.*

---

18.   What did Jesus' disciple Thomas call Him?

*John 20:28—And Thomas answered and said unto him, **My Lord and my God.***

---

19.   Would it be robbery to God's glory for any man to claim to be God's equal?

---

20.   Was it robbery for Jesus to claim to be equal with God? Why?

*Philippians 2:6–7—Who [Christ], being in the form of God, **thought it not robbery to be equal with God**: but made himself of no reputation, and took upon him the form of a servant, and was made in the likeness of men.*

It was not robbery because He is God. John 1:1–3 and verse 14 teach that Jesus is God and was in heaven from the beginning of time.

GOD'S EXCHANGE

Jesus left the splendor and perfection of heaven, and took on the body of a man and lived on earth so that He could die as the perfect **substitute** for our sin penalty. When the Bible states, "God so loved the world," it means every man and woman in the world. Jesus became a man so that He could give His life in **exchange** for every person who has sinned.

OUR SUBSTITUTE

All this means *He loves you in particular* and has given Himself as your substitute.

21. What does this verse teach that Jesus did with our sins?

> *1 Peter 2:24—***Who his own self [Jesus] bare our sins in his own body on the tree,** *that we, being dead to sins, should live unto righteousness: by whose stripes [punishment you] were healed.*

_____

22. Describe the exchange Jesus offered through His suffering. Why did He make such an exchange?

> *1 Peter 3:18—Christ also hath once suffered for sins,* **the just for the unjust, that he might bring us to God***.*

_____

_____

As the holy/just God Who came in human form, He is the only One qualified to die in your place. He took your sins on Himself when He died on the cross.

OUR RIGHTEOUSNESS

He dealt with your sinful record thoroughly, but He also offers His own record to you as a perfect completion to the exchange.

23. Describe the nature of the exchange as it is referred to in this verse.

*2 Corinthians 5:21—For he [**God has**] **made** him [**Jesus**] **to be sin for us**, who knew no sin; **that we might be made the righteousness of God in him.***

_____

_____

When we take His offer, we take His righteous record and meet His holy standard. Now God can give us a home with Him in heaven forever and still be just.

Write your name in the blank below

_____'s Record	Jesus' Record
Lying	Holy
Stealing	Just
Coveting	Accepted by God
And so forth	Free to live with God

Now cross out your name and write *Jesus*. Cross out Jesus' name and write your own.

This is the reality of the exchange He offers us! He suffered as a lying, coveting thief in your place and offers you the ability to have a full relationship with God, as your Father, accepted by Him because of Jesus' holy, just nature.

OUR FULL PAYMENT

You may be thinking, "I see that, but surely I must do something!"

24. Does Christ's death cover all your past sins?

> *1 John 1:7—The blood of Jesus Christ his Son [cleanses] us from all sin.*

_____

Does it cover all your present, and even future, sins?

_____

The Bible says **all**! Of course it means all your sins. You may be saying to yourself, "Yes, but I still have to keep myself from sinning to stay forgiven. It can't mean my future sins." Think about this. All your sins were future when Jesus died. He forgave all your sins—past, present, and even future!

25. What did Jesus mean when He cried these words from the cross?

> *John 19:30—When Jesus therefore had received the vinegar, he said, **It is finished**: and he bowed his head, and gave up the ghost [chose to die].*

_____

The word *finished* in the original language is *tetelestai* and means **"Paid in full!"**

If it was paid in full, is there anything left for you to pay?

No! Jesus paid it all for you! We don't have to provide anything to save ourselves from our own sin penalty. He did all the saving!

26. What does the Bible say happened to Christ after He died for our sins?

> *1 Corinthians 15:3–4—Christ died for our sins . . . and . . . **was buried**, and . . . **he rose again** the third day according to the scriptures.*

27. Circle the words *He was seen* in the passage below, which refers to the time immediately following His resurrection (you should find them four times).

> *1 Corinthians 15:5–8—And that he was seen of Cephas, then of the twelve: after that, he was seen of above five hundred brethren at once; of whom the greater part remain unto this present, but some are fallen asleep [dead]. After that, he was seen of James; then of all the apostles. And last of all he was seen of me also, as of one born out of due time.*

Jesus proved that He was indeed powerful enough to win the victory over sin and its penalty—death and hell. He rose from the grave and was seen by over five hundred eyewitnesses. His resurrection also proved that God was satisfied with His payment for our sins. He loves, much more than most people suspect, and His love is powerful enough to reach even you and me! It's true! Jesus really is God. He really did leave heaven's splendor to be born of a virgin, live a perfect life, and die in your place. And it is true that He really rose from the grave, defeating sin, death, and hell for you.

Do you believe this? _____

SUMMARY

When Jesus was on earth, He told a touching story that clearly shows God's love. It is the story of the prodigal son found in Luke 15:11–24. Many will identify with the son in this retelling of the story.

There was a very wealthy man who had two sons. The younger of the two came to his father one day and demanded his half of the inheritance he was sure he would get some day. No doubt the father was brokenhearted, but he did not attempt to force the young man to love him. He decided to divide his wealth between his two sons. It wasn't very long afterward that the youngest son liquidated his assets and took a trip far away from his home. Who knows why? Perhaps he was jealous of his brother, perhaps he was embittered by his father's insistence on rules; but whatever the case, he had his freedom and he was going to spend that freedom, and spend it he did.

Reports traveled back to the father that the wayward son was living one long riot—hiring prostitutes, buying friends, and wasting all his money. When the money was gone, there came a great famine that caused an economic depression in the region where he had traveled, and the young man was destitute. He couldn't find work, and when he did finally get a job slopping hogs, it didn't even pay enough for him to eat.

One day while he was feeding the pigs, he was so hungry he found himself daydreaming about how good it would be to have the hogs' slop to eat. It was at this low point that he "came to himself" and realized what a fool he had been. He began to talk to himself out loud. "How many servants does my father have? They have food to waste and here I am literally dying of hunger!"

With a resolve in his voice and hope in his heart for the first time in a long time, he said, "I'm going home to face Dad! I'll say to him, 'Dad, I've done wrong. I've sinned against God and against you. I don't deserve to be your son anymore, but if you'll have me, I'd like to become one of your servants.'"

Hearing himself say those words gave him the courage to take the first few steps. After that his heart was light as he hurried home.

Several days later, weak from hunger, he found himself only a mile from home. Just around the corner he would be able to see the front porch of the giant old house. Now he was frightened. What would his father say? Would he accept his apology? With those last few thoughts he rounded the bend. He stopped in his tracks and allowed his hungry eyes to drink in the beautiful sight. There was the old tree and the place where he and his brother used to play, and there was the house! Oh, how good it all looked. And then his heart skipped a beat when he realized that there was someone standing on the porch. There was a wave, and a faltering move toward him, and then he heard it across the way. His father was calling out his name.

It was a long way across the huge estate, but his father was running toward him the best that he could. He rehearsed the words he was going to say one more time. He wasn't prepared for what happened next. He felt the warm embrace of his father as he fell on him. The feeling was so warm and secure. It was as if he were a little boy again and everything was okay. His weary soul luxuriated in the warmth of that embrace. He and his father reluctantly stepped back and stood at arms length looking each other over. There he was face to face with his father. There was an awkward silent moment, and finally he heard himself saying, "Dad, I've done wrong. I've sinned against God and against you. I don't deserve to be your son anymore, but if . . ."

His father interrupted him. What the son didn't know was that his father had been on that porch for days watching and waiting for this very moment. His heart was burning with compassion as he called to the servants, "Bring forth the best robe in the house and dress this boy in something proper; and bring a family ring. Put it back on his hand; and he'll need some shoes."

Standing there with tears streaming down his face, looking at the weak, emaciated form of his son, he added, "Bring out the fatted calf, and kill it. Let's eat, and be happy again, for this my son was dead, and is alive now. He was lost, and is found." The father, the son, and the whole house began to be merry.

Friend, this is a picture of God's attitude toward **you**. Your sin and His perfect nature have driven you apart. He can't tolerate or overlook your sin, but He longs to forgive you through the substitutionary death of His own dear Son. He is watching and waiting for you to admit your sin and seek His forgiveness.

Lesson 4 deals with how to access this forgiveness. If you don't want to wait until then, please ask your Bible study leader to show you now—from the Bible.

APPLICATION

If you were going to talk to God about what you have learned in this Bible study, what would you tell Him?

_____

_____

_____

_____

MEMORIZE

John 3:16—For God so loved the world that he gave his only begotten Son, that [whoever believes] in him should not perish, but have everlasting life.

PRACTICAL ASSIGNMENT

Read these additional verses about God's love for you and write your own words of appreciation to Him.

*2 Corinthians 5:14—For **the love of Christ [constrains] us**; because we thus judge, that if one died for all, then were all dead.*

*Galatians 2:20—I am crucified with Christ: nevertheless I live; yet not I, but Christ [lives] in me: and the life which I now live in the flesh I live by the faith of **the Son of God, who loved me, and gave himself for me**.*

*Ephesians 5:2—And walk in **love**, as Christ also **[has] loved us, and [has] given himself for us an offering and a sacrifice to God** for a sweet smelling savour [fragrance].*

*1 John 3:1—**Behold, what manner of love the Father [has] bestowed upon us**, that we should be called the sons of God.*

*1 John 3:16—Hereby perceive we the **love of God**, because **he laid down his life for us**.*

*1 John 4:9—In this was manifested [demonstrated] the **love of God** toward us, because that **God sent His only begotten Son into the world**, that we might live through Him.*

*1 John 4:10—Herein is **love**, not that we loved God, but that **he loved us, and sent his Son to be the propitiation** [satisfaction for justice] **for our sins**.*

*Revelation 1:5—And from **Jesus Christ**, who is the faithful witness, and the first begotten of the dead, and the prince of the kings of the earth. Unto him that **loved us, and washed us from our sins in his own blood**.*

_____

_____

_____

_____

_____

_____

_____

In the space provided record any ongoing questions about God that you may have. Be sure to show them to your Bible study leader so that you will be able to discuss them together.

_____

_____

_____

_____

If you started reading a chapter a day in the book of John, continue reading. Ask God to speak to you as you read His book. Since He is real, He can do that. Don't expect Him to speak out loud to you, but you can expect Him to speak to you. He promises that He will convince you in your heart of certain truths about Himself and about you. It will not be an audible voice, but there will be a growing awareness that what the Bible says is true! You may even sense a tugging or a squeezing in your heart. That is the Lord!

In the space remaining, also record any verses that seem to stand out to you or any questions you have as you read.

_____

_____

_____

_____

_____

_____

_____

_____

_____

_____

LESSON 4

GOD IS GRACIOUS AND MAN IS NEEDY

So far we have seen that God is holy and cannot tolerate our sin, He is just and cannot overlook our sin, and He is love and cannot ignore our problem. His love compelled Him to send Jesus to live a perfect life and die in our place as payment for our sin. The transfer of this payment of sin can be applied to our need only through a gift. We can do nothing to earn it. This gift from God is called grace. This lesson is about the marvelous grace of God and how we can access that grace through faith.

1. God's holy and just nature keeps Him from simply clearing the guilty. What part of His character caused Him to seek a way to forgive our guilt?

    *Numbers 14:18—**The Lord** is longsuffering [slow to anger], and **of great mercy**, forgiving iniquity [sin] and transgression [breaking God's law], and by no means clearing the guilty.*

2. In lesson 2 we saw that God is prepared to judge our sin. What else is He ready to do? Why?

    *Nehemiah 9:17—**Thou art a God ready to pardon, gracious and merciful**, slow to anger, and of great kindness.*

    _____

    Grace is God giving to man what he does not deserve. Mercy is God not giving to man what he does deserve. Do you remember what men deserve because of their sins? _____

3. God's mercy delivered the person who wrote Psalm 86 from an eternal consequence. What was it?

    *Psalm 86:13—For great is **thy mercy toward me: and thou hast delivered my soul from the lowest hell**.*

    _____

4. Why is God willing to hear our prayers?

    *Exodus 22:27—And it shall come to pass, when he [cries] unto me [God], that I will hear; **for I am gracious**.*

    _____

5. How did God's grace become available to mankind?

    *John 1:17—For the law was given by Moses, but **grace** and truth **came by Jesus Christ**.*

    _____

6. To whom does God make His grace available?

    *Titus 2:11—For **the grace of God** that brings salvation [has] **appeared** [been made visible] **to all men**.*

    _____

7. Grace was given to mankind as a gift from God. Who paid the price for God's grace?

    2 Corinthians 8:9—For [you] know the grace of our Lord Jesus Christ, that, **though he was rich, yet for your sakes he became poor, that [you] through his poverty might be rich***.*

    _____

8. How do we gain access to the gift of God's grace?

    Romans 5:1–2—Therefore being **justified by faith***, we have peace with God through our Lord Jesus Christ: by whom also* **we have access by faith into** *this* **grace***.*

    _____

9. The words *faith* and *believe* mean the same thing. Record the promise associated with believing found in each of these verses.

    Acts 10:43—Through his [Jesus'] name **whosoever [believes] in him shall receive remission** *[forgiveness]* **of sins***.*

    _____

    Romans 10:4—For Christ is the end [fulfillment] of the law for **righteousness to every one that [believes]***.*

    _____

    John 6:47—Verily, verily, [Truly, truly] I [Jesus] say unto you, **he that [believes] on me [has] everlasting life***.*

    _____

Christ provided forgiveness of sins, His perfect righteousness placed to our account, and eternal life in heaven when He died and rose again. All this is available to each person on earth through God's grace and is accessed by faith. Since faith determines so much, it is necessary for us to define it clearly.

10. What do you say faith is?

_____

_____

COMMON FAITH

I have found that a common answer to this question of what is faith is to understand and to agree. It makes sense that no one can believe something until he or she understands it, but clearly understanding is not enough. I understand the premise of many things with which I do not agree. However, knowing about Christ intellectually and agreeing in your heart that what you know is true is still not enough.

11. Did the demons in this passage know and agree that Christ is the Son of God?

> Luke 4:41—And devils also came out of many, crying out, and saying, **Thou [Jesus] art Christ the Son of God . . . for they knew that he was Christ**.

_____

Demons understand that Jesus is the Son of God, Who died and rose again, and they agree with this reality; but obviously they are not on their way to heaven.

SAVING FAITH

By saving faith, I mean the kind of faith that accesses God's grace. Saving faith has three elements. It's just like the angles of a triangle, or the legs of a three-legged stool, where every angle or leg is essential. Even so, saving faith is not saving if it is not complete. The first two angles of saving faith are found in common faith. (1) You must understand that you have sinned and deserve the judgment of hell, and you must also understand that Jesus paid your penalty through His death and resurrection. (2) You must agree in your heart that this is truth. The first two angles deal with the mind and emotions, but the third is a decision involving the will. (3) You must choose to depend on Jesus Christ to become your personal Savior from sin and hell.

In 1859, the famous acrobat Charles Blondine stretched a tightrope 190 feet above the waters of Niagara Falls. Crowds gathered daily as he navigated the thousand-foot span. He walked across in a large burlap bag. He carried his manager across on his back. He even fitted a special wheelbarrow for the rope and pushed it across. Once, he put a cookstove in the wheelbarrow and stopped in the middle of the rope to cook and eat an omelet. The story is told that once while working with the wheelbarrow, he approached the cheering crowd and asked them who believed he could put a man in the wheelbarrow and take him across. The crowd went wild. Everyone wanted to see that stunt. They began to chant, "I believe, I believe, I believe!"

Blondine pointed to a man waving his hand and chanting, "I believe, I believe!" He said to the man, "You, sir, get in the wheelbarrow."

The man bolted in the other direction. What was wrong? The man believed that Blondine could put a man, some other man, into the wheelbarrow, but he wasn't willing to place his dependence on Blondine to take him across.

This third angle of saving faith is the angle that many people neglect. They believe that Jesus lived and died and agree that this is good, but they still believe they need to do something to earn favor with God. They are depending on their good works. They believe they have to be good to their fellow man, they try to obey God's law, and so forth.

12. Is it possible to satisfy God's holiness and justice through our own abilities?

   *Romans 3:20—Therefore by the **deeds of the law there shall no flesh be justified** in his sight: for by the law is the knowledge of sin.*

   _____

13. The law was given to show us that we are sinners and that we need a Savior. Where does the Bible say we find favor with God?

   *Romans 3:24—**Being justified freely by his grace** through the redemption [purchase of freedom] **that is in Christ Jesus**.*

   _____

14. What conclusion does the Bible come to concerning the place of our own good works in receiving grace?

   *Romans 4:4–5, 16—Now to him that [works] is the reward not reckoned of grace, but of debt. But **to him that [works] not, but [believes]** on him that [justifies] the ungodly, his faith is counted for righteousness. . . . Therefore it is of faith, that it might be by grace.*

   _____

15. Since receiving salvation from sin and death is by grace, then what is it not by?

   *Romans 11:6—And if by grace, **then is it no more of works**: otherwise grace is no more grace. But if it be of* *works, then is it no more grace: otherwise work is no more work.*

---

16. Note the two words that are involved in salvation from sin and hell. Do either of these words involve anything **we** do?

    *Titus 3:5—**Not by works** of righteousness which we have done, but **according to his mercy he saved us**, by the washing of regeneration, and renewing of the Holy Ghost [Spirit].*

    *Ephesians 2:8–9—**For by grace are [you] saved** through faith; and that not of yourselves: it is the gift of God: **not of works**, lest any man should boast.*

---

17. Some might still say they want to add their own good works to their faith just to be sure. What does the Bible say about adding works to what you depend on for salvation?

    *Romans 3:28—Therefore we conclude that a man is **justified by faith without the deeds of the law.***

Imagine two chairs sitting side by side. The one on the left represents you and your efforts to get to heaven on your own, and the one on the right represents the finished payment of Christ for all your sins. If you are sitting in the chair representing self, what do you have to do to transfer your dependence to the chair representing Christ? You have to get out of the one chair and sit in the other. In order to transfer your dependence to God's grace for salvation, you have to stop depending on what you can do. It is a decision. Just like someone would have had to get in Blondine's wheelbarrow to demonstrate real dependence on his ability to take him or her across, even so you have to decide to trust Jesus alone to give you eternal life in heaven.

What if a person decides to sit in both chairs? Is he really trusting either chair? No! When a person tries to trust in Jesus and his own efforts, he shows that he doubts that Jesus is enough. Saving faith is choosing to trust Christ's payment for sin as your own payment and nothing else. It's like a transaction. You choose to trust in what Christ has already done for you on the cross, and He gives to you forgiveness of sins, credited righteousness, and eternal life.

18.   What is another Bible word for this decision?

Luke 13:3—I tell you, Nay: but, except [you] **repent***, [you] shall all likewise perish.*

_____

The word *repent* means to change your mind. Maybe you have been thinking that your sins are not bad enough to condemn you to hell. *You will have to change your mind about that.* Perhaps you have been thinking that your own good works will outweigh your sins and get you to heaven. *You will have to change your mind about that.* The decision you need to make is simple. Recognize your need, stop depending on yourself and your own efforts, and start depending on the finished work of Christ.

SUMMARY

There is a point of no return on the Niagara River, where the current from the falls is too powerful for a boat to navigate safely. It's marked clearly with warnings, because if a boat goes past that point, it is bound to be pulled by the current over the roaring falls. Imagine a man in a rowboat absentmindedly crossing that line. When he realizes what he has done, he tries to turn back to safety, but it is too late. No matter how hard he rows, he is still being pulled inch by inch closer to impending doom. Suppose someone on the shore sees his plight and expertly throws a rope across his lap. Now he has a choice to make. Will he keep up his own efforts only to eventually plunge to sure destruction, or will he drop the oars of self-effort and trust the rope of safety? What would you do?

19. What does the Bible say is necessary to receive God's grace?

*James 4:6—**God** [resists, fights against] the proud, but [**gives**] **grace unto the humble**.*

_____

Will you humble yourself and admit that you have sinned and that your sin is an offense to our holy God? Will you admit that you can't save yourself from His justice? Will you humble yourself and trust the loving gift of His sacrifice, which He longs to give you? Will you humble yourself and place your dependence on Him alone for eternal life and forgiveness of sins?

If your answer is yes, tell Him right now in a prayer.

Record below what you told Him.

_____

_____

_____

_____

_____

_____

Here is a sample prayer. You can pray this in your heart if you really mean it. Remember, it is not about praying the right words, but choosing to depend on God. The choice to believe is what accesses His saving grace.

> Dear Jesus, I have sinned against Your holy nature and deserve judgment in hell. I believe that You loved me enough to die in my place. Please forgive my sins, exchange my sinful record for Your holy one, and give me eternal life in heaven. Right now, I place my dependence on You alone for salvation. Thank You, Jesus. Amen

20. Did you transfer your dependence to Jesus alone to save you from sin and hell?

   _____

21. Based on what you have seen in His Word, if you were to die right now where would you go? (Remember God cannot lie.)

   _____

22. If you were to die five years from now, where would you go?

   _____

Remember, it's not about what you feel or even what you think. It's about what God has promised. Look back at question 9 to see what He promised to do if you decide to believe. If you have decided to depend on Him for grace, He has given you everlasting life. How long is everlasting? _____

How long will you have His forgiveness of sins, righteousness, and eternal life?

_____

23. If you had died yesterday, or before you made this decision, where would you have gone?

_____

Remember Revelation 20:14 says, "And death and hell were cast into the lake of fire. This is the second death." You see, this decision has made a huge difference, hasn't it.

24. Were you guilty before you made this decision?

_____

25. Are you guilty now?

_____

Remember the promises!

> *Psalm 103:12—As far as the east is from the west, so far has he [God] removed our transgressions [breaking God's law] from us.*

South will meet north at the poles, but you can travel east for twenty years and you will never go west. They never meet! That is how far removed your guilt is! You have heard the Truth and the Truth has set you FREE!

APPLICATION

If you were going to talk to God about what you have learned in this Bible study, what would you tell Him?

_____

_____

_____

MEMORIZE

John 6:47—Verily, verily [Truly, truly] I [Jesus] say unto you, He that [believes] on me [has] everlasting life.

PRACTICAL ASSIGNMENT

If you have made this decision, why don't you call your Bible study leader right now and tell him or her, who will be very happy and will want to rejoice with you.

Read these verses to see if you can determine Who else is rejoicing with you.

> *Luke 15:7—I say unto you, that . . . joy shall be in heaven over one sinner that [repents], more than over ninety and nine just persons, which need no repentance.*
>
> *Luke 15:10—I say unto you, there is joy in the presence of the angels of God over one sinner that [repents].*
>
> *Luke 15:24—For this my son was dead, and is alive again; he was lost, and is found.*

26. Who is in heaven with the angels?

_____

Right now, God Himself is rejoicing that you have come home to Him.

In the space provided record any ongoing questions about God you may have. Be sure to show them to your Bible study leader so that you will be able to discuss them together.

_____

_____

_____

_____

_____

If you started reading a chapter a day in the book of John, continue reading. Ask God to speak to you as you read His book. Since He is real, He can do that. Don't expect Him to speak out loud to you, but you can expect Him to speak to you. He promises that He will convince you in your heart of certain truths about Himself and about you. It will not be an audible voice but a growing awareness that what the Bible says is true! You may even sense a tugging or a squeezing in your heart. That is the Lord!

In the space remaining, also record any verses that seem to stand out to you or any questions you have as you read.

_____

_____

_____

_____

_____

LIVING THE EXCHANGE

Living the Exchange is a twelve-lesson Bible study that will help you as you begin to live this new life in Christ. Now that you have begun a close relationship with God, you need to learn to live. Learn to live with Him as your Father, Master, Lord and King, friend and partner. He is such a loving, giving Lord. Don't you want to start right away? Please talk to your Bible study leader about *Living the Exchange*.